Copyright © 2023 Philip Lumbang.

All rights reserved. This book or any portion thereof may not be reproduced or used in any manner whatsoever without the express written permission of the publisher except for the use of brief quotations in a book review.

Printed by Amazon, Inc., in the United States of America.

The AI Alphabet

An AI-powered journey through the alphabet

Written and Illustrated by:
P.J. Midchat

"For the future generations"

A is for Artificial Intelligence,
The technology that's really wise.

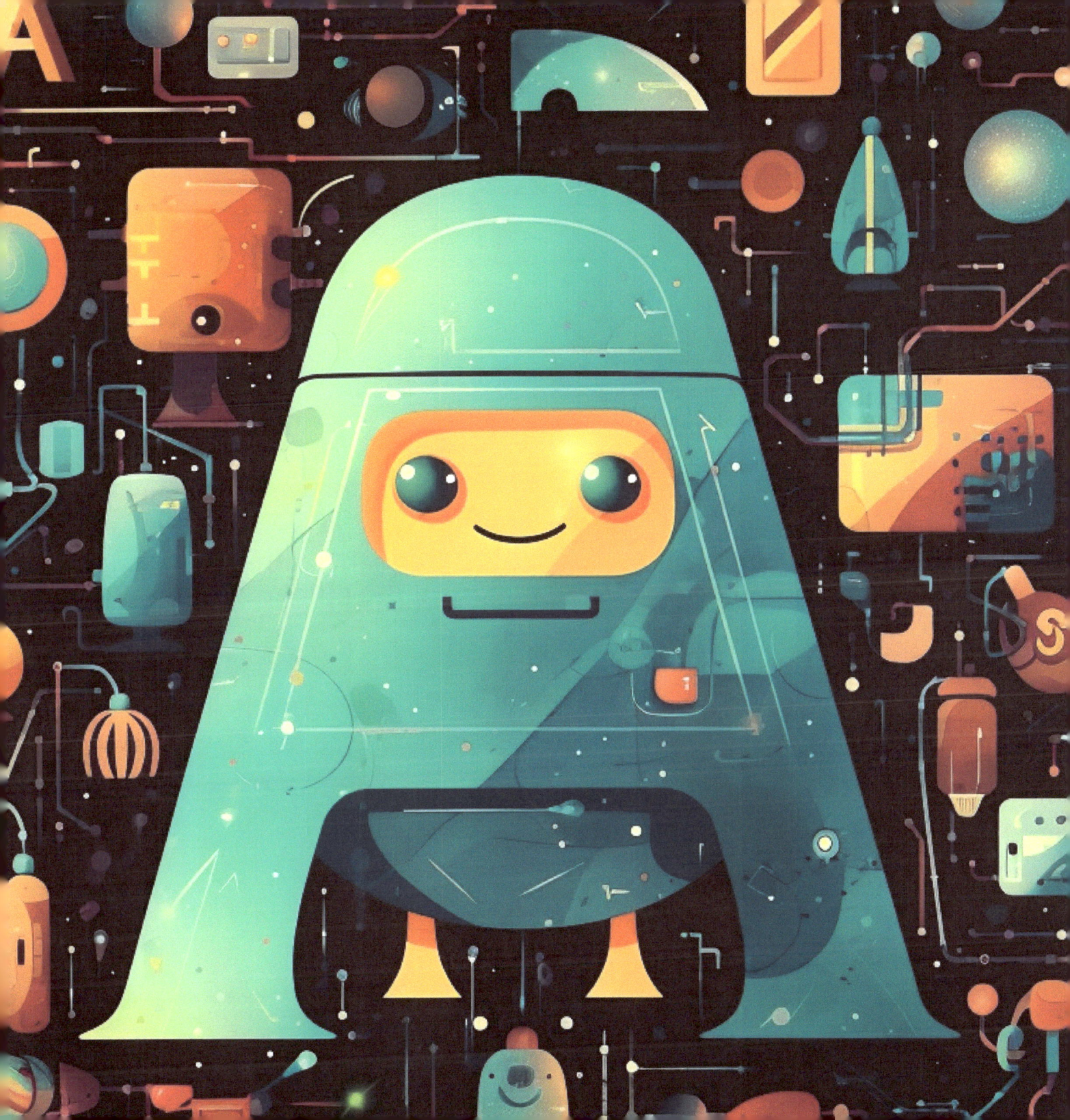

B is for Bot, a machine that can talk,
It can chat with you around the clock.

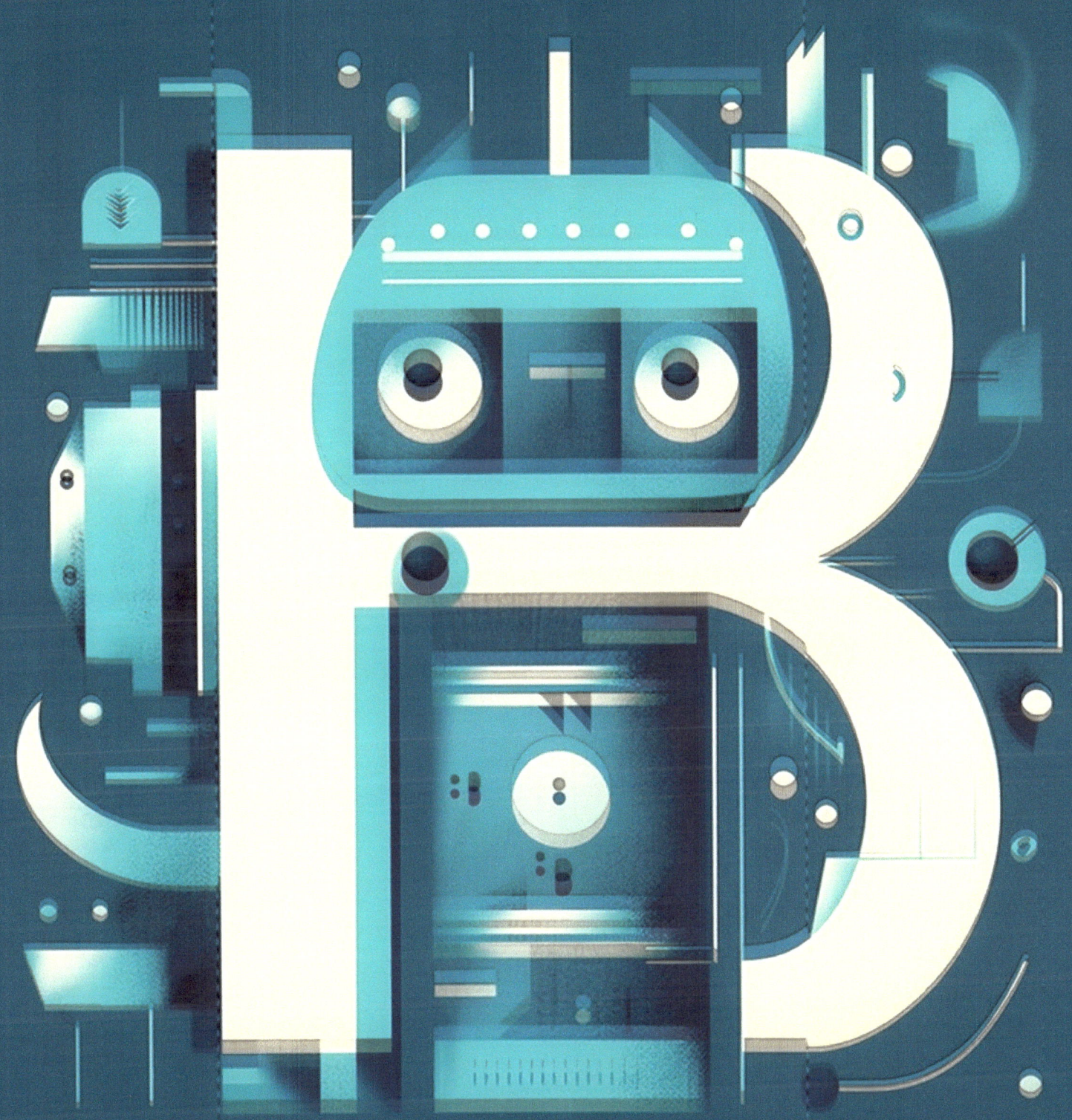

C is for Code, the language we use,
To program machines, and make them do.

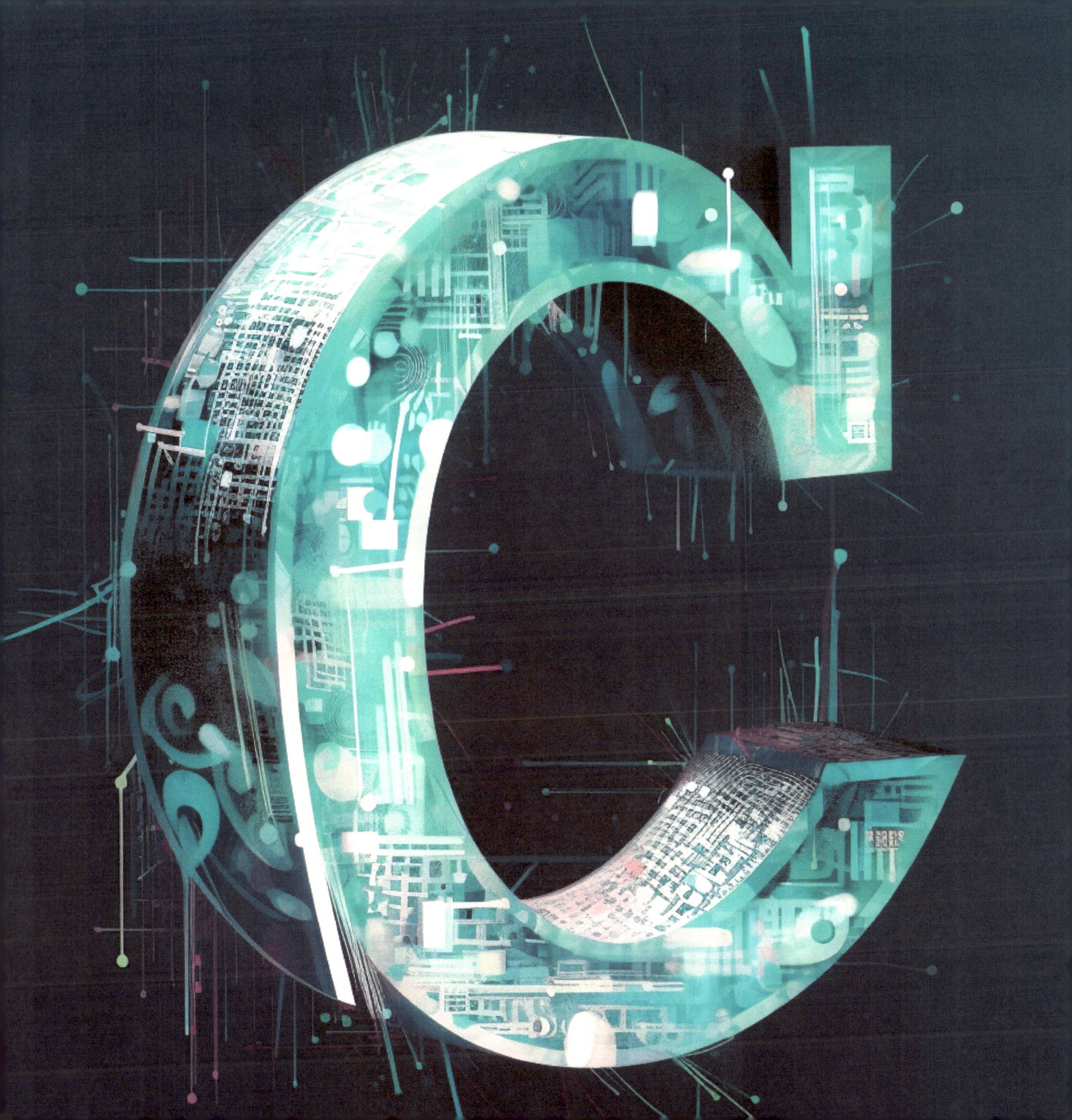

D is for Data, the information we feed,
To AI systems, so they can proceed.

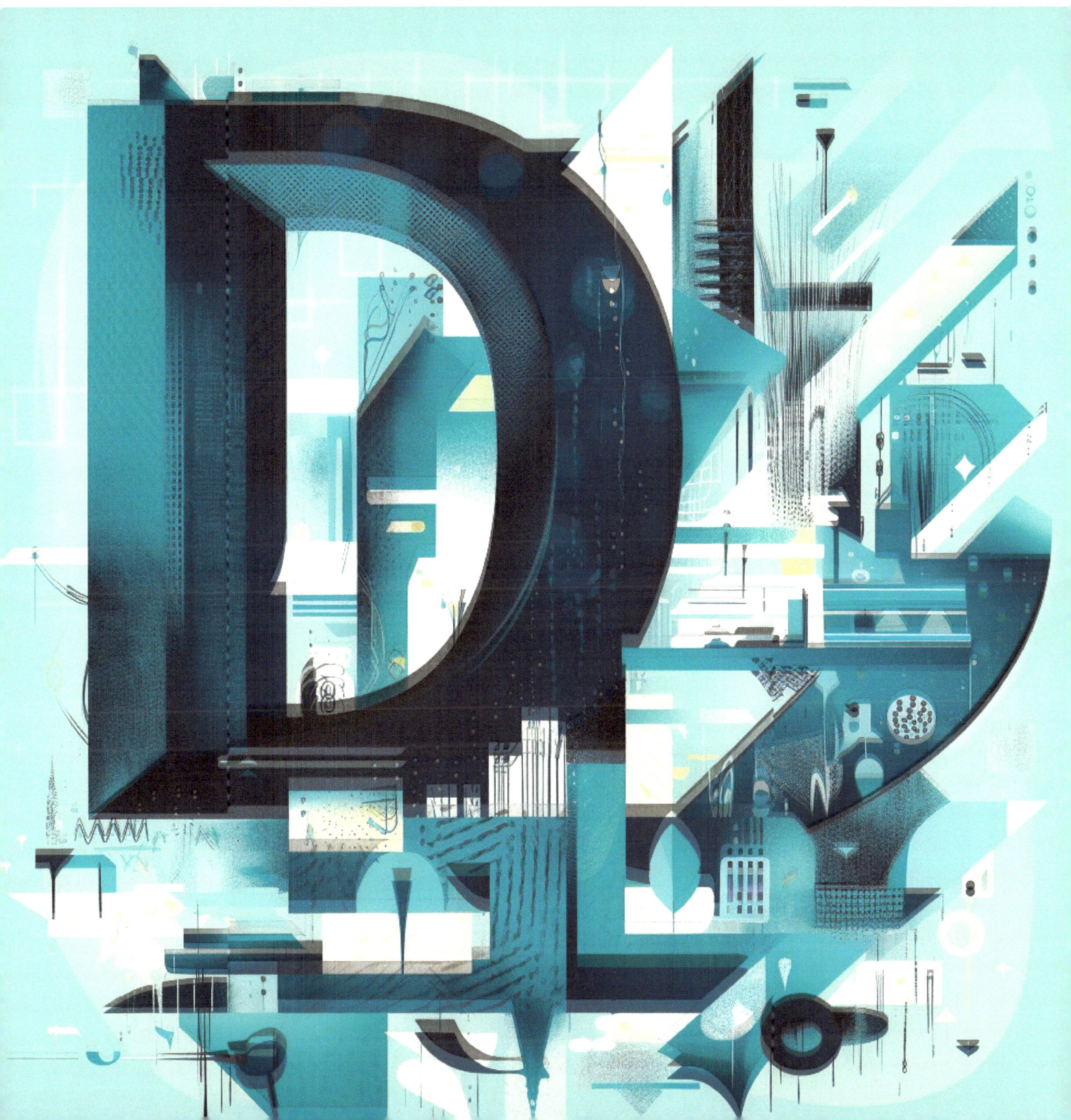

E is for Expert System, a program so smart,
It can solve problems, and play its part.

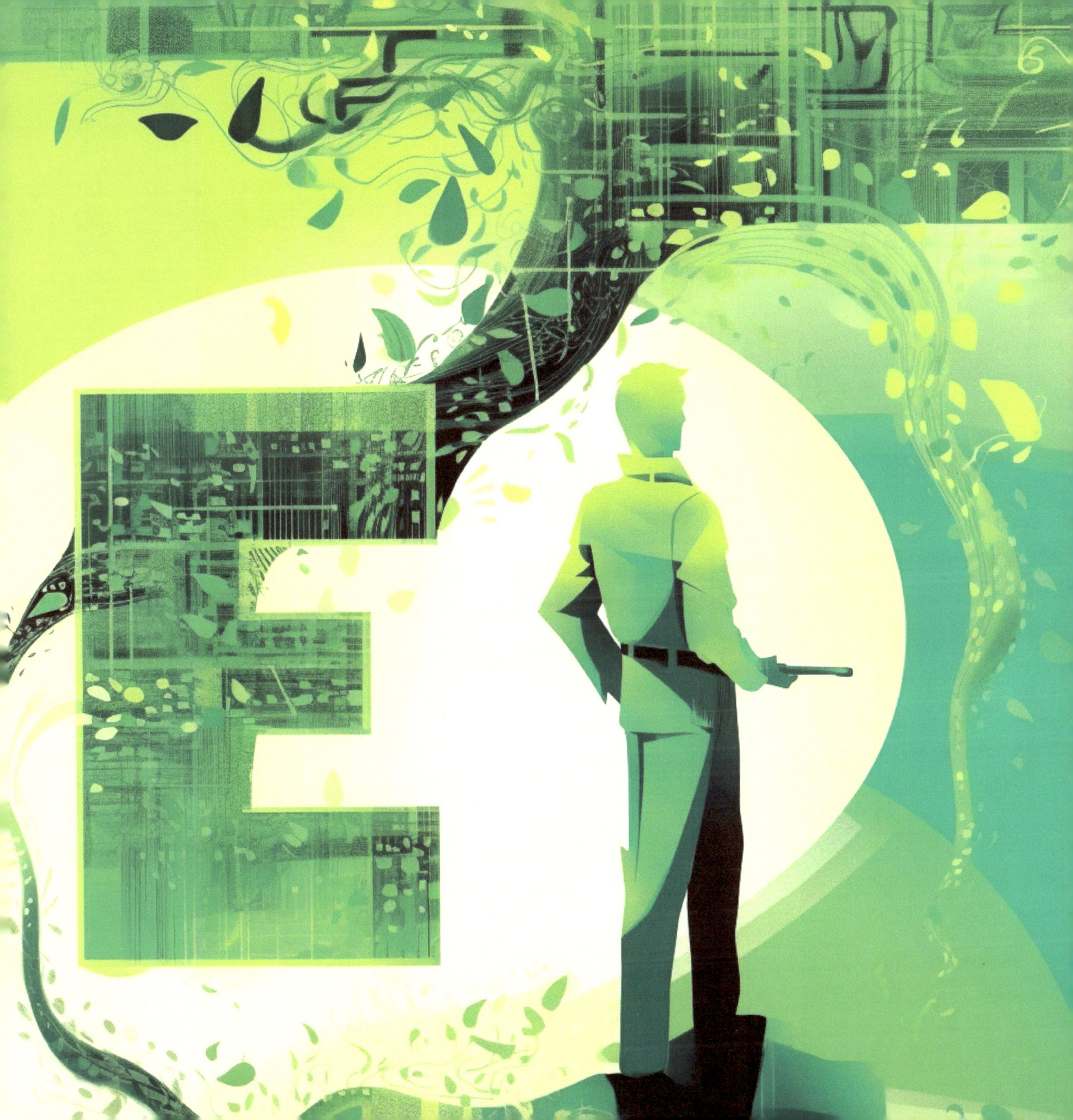

F is for Facial Recognition,
AI can detect faces, with great precision.

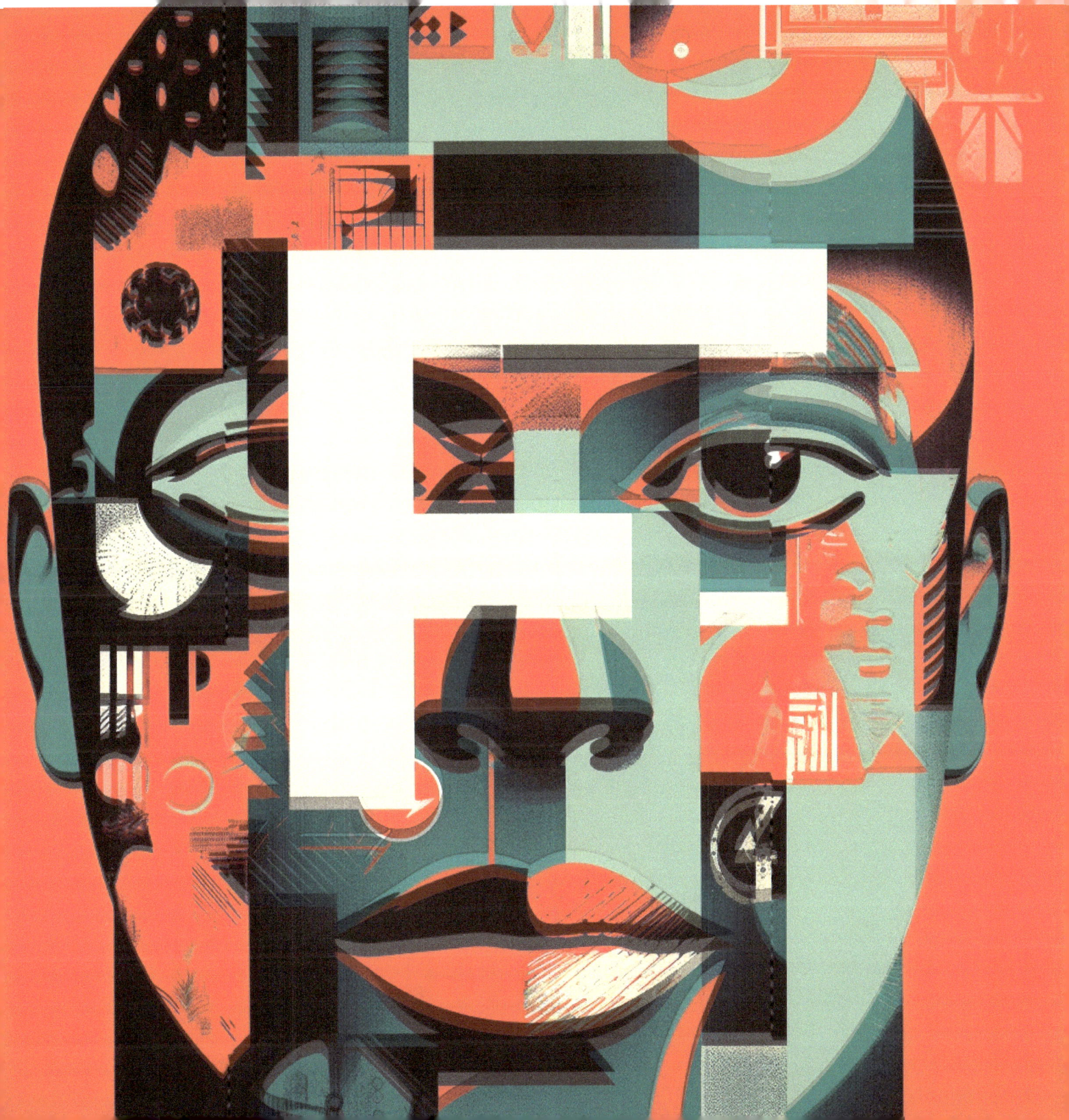

G is for Gaming, AI can compete,
It can beat humans, and sweep the heat.

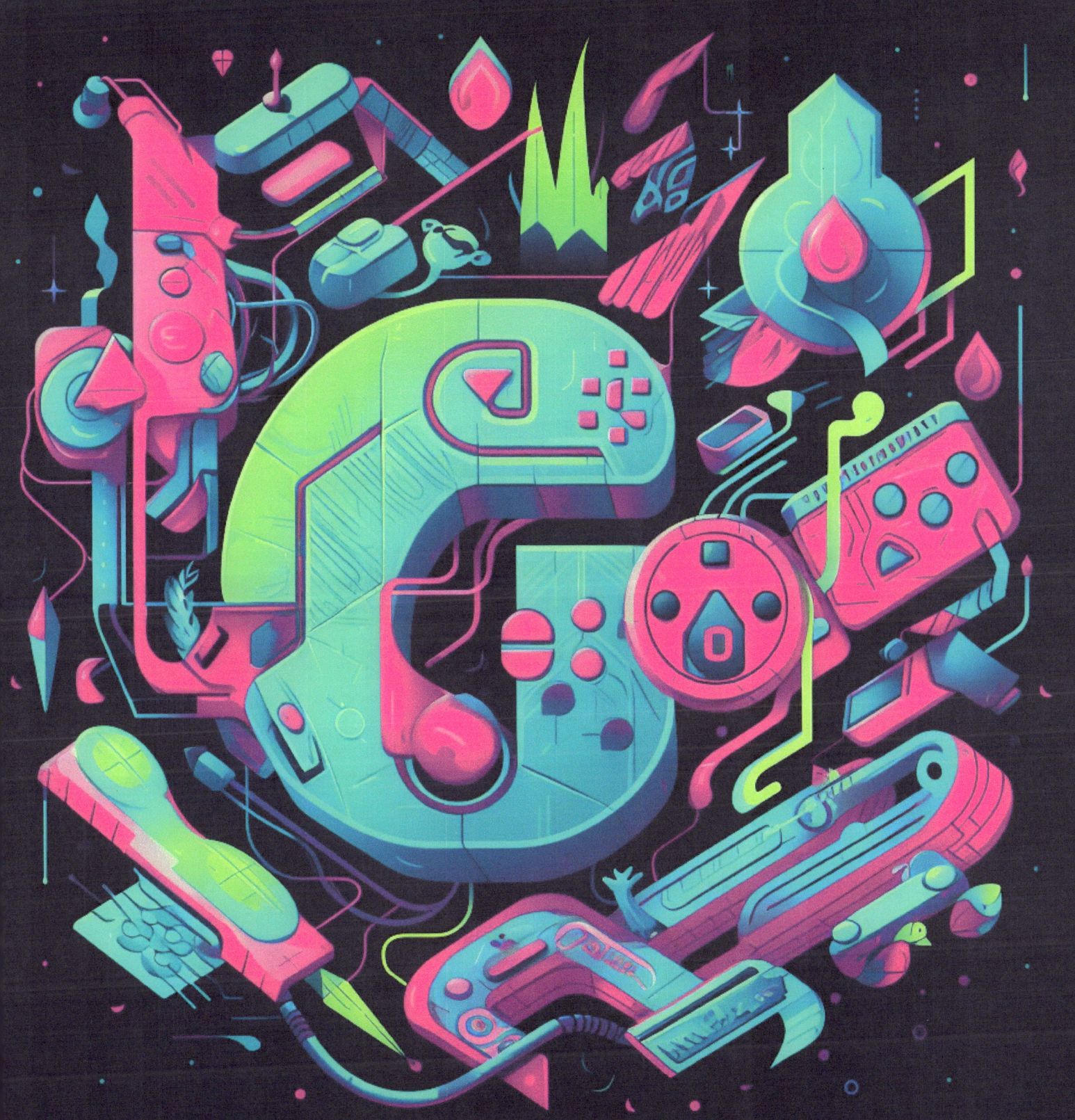

H is for Humanoid Robots,
AI machines with hands and feet.

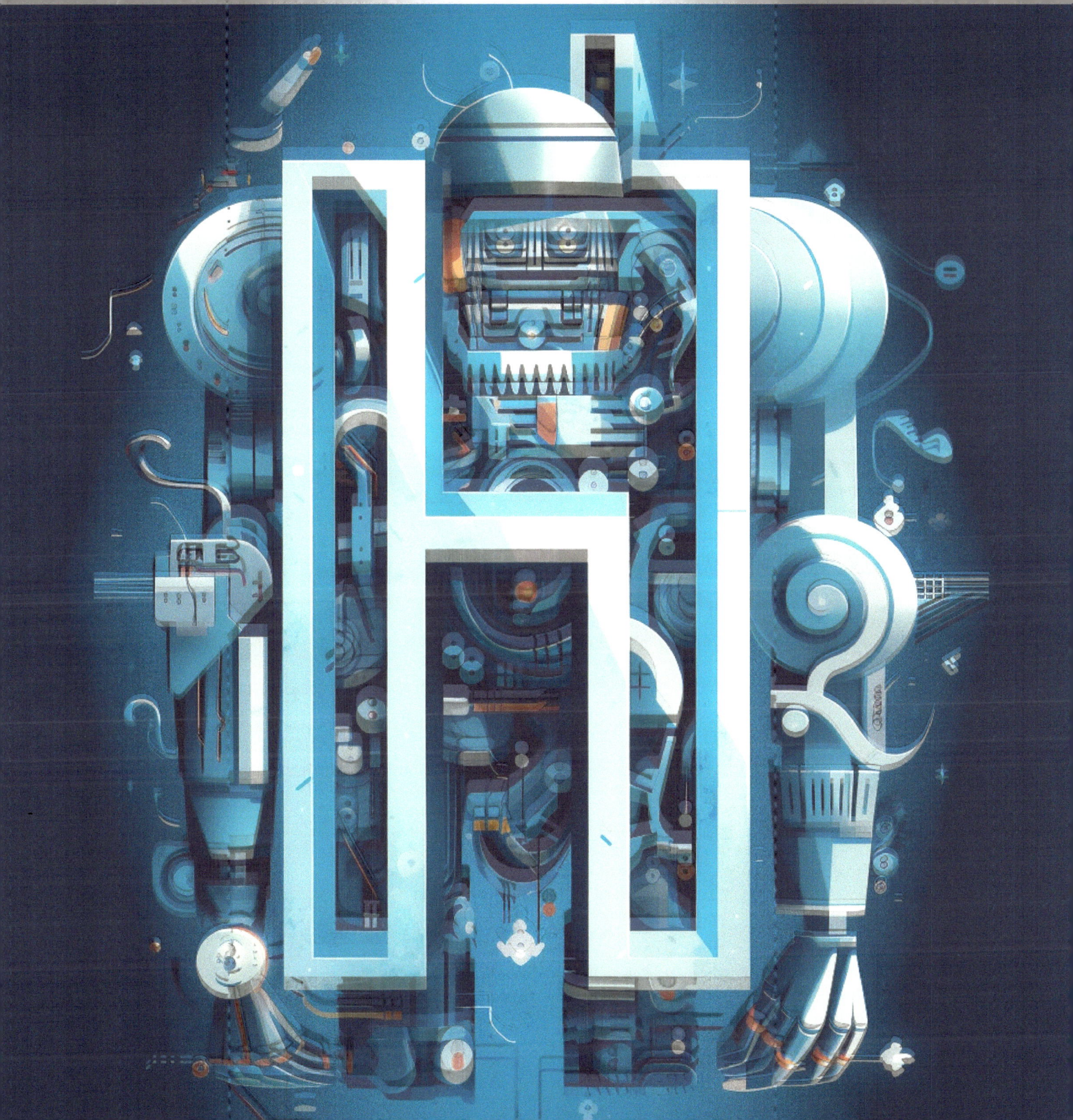

I is for Intelligence, the ability to learn,
AI can improve, with each new turn.

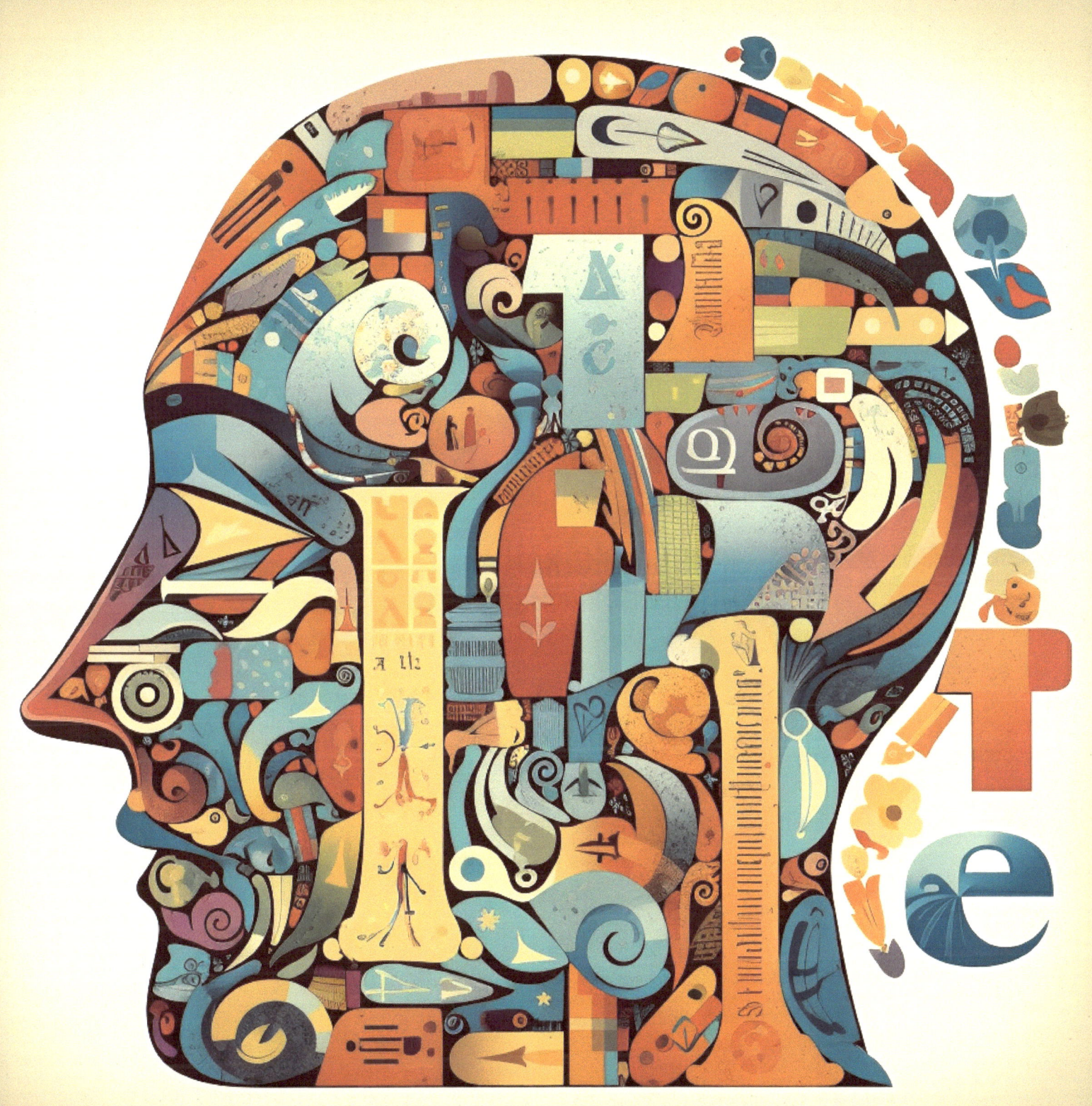

J is for Job Automation,
AI can do tasks with great dedication.

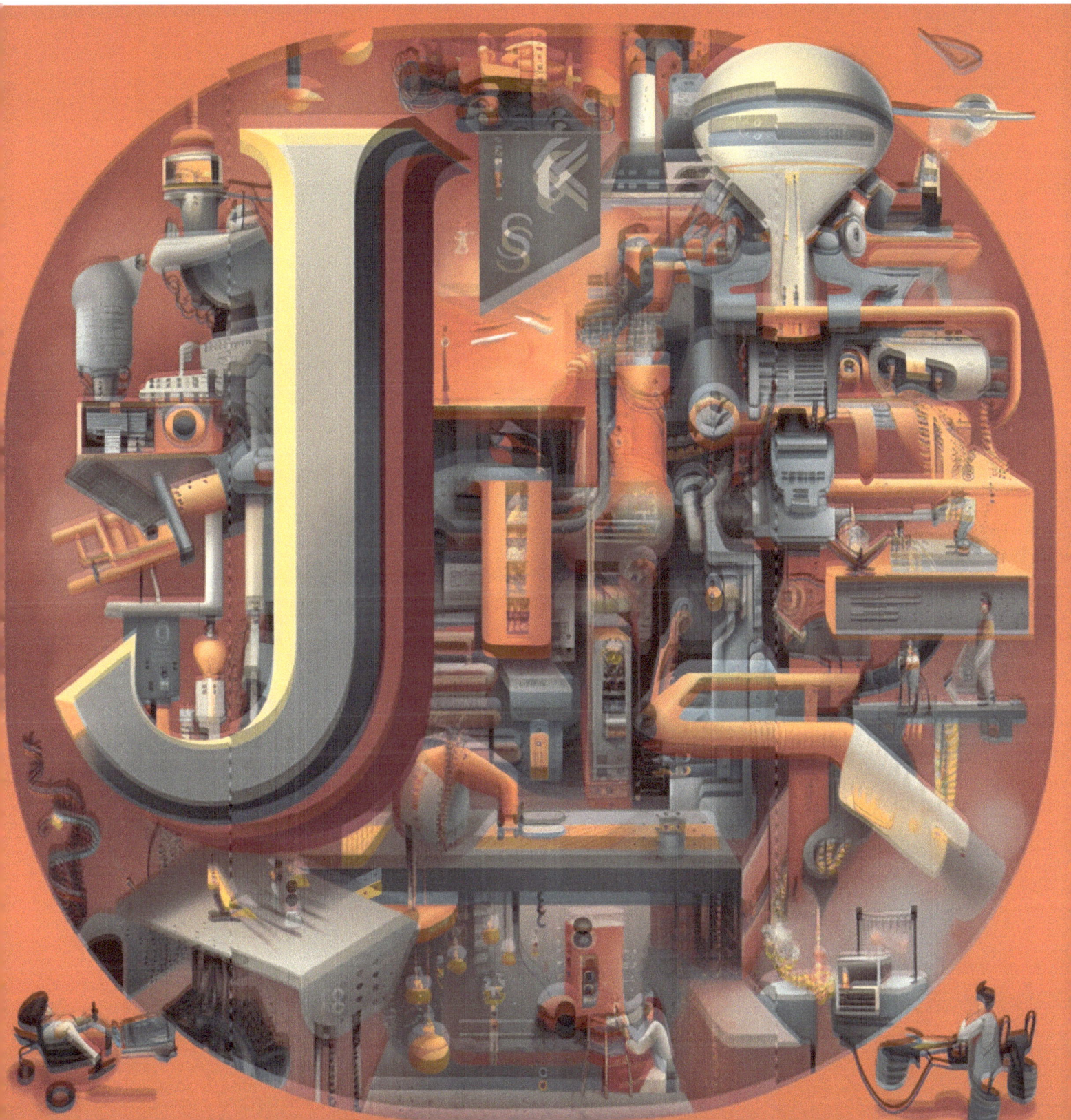

K is for Knowledge, AI can gain,
It can learn from data, and retain.

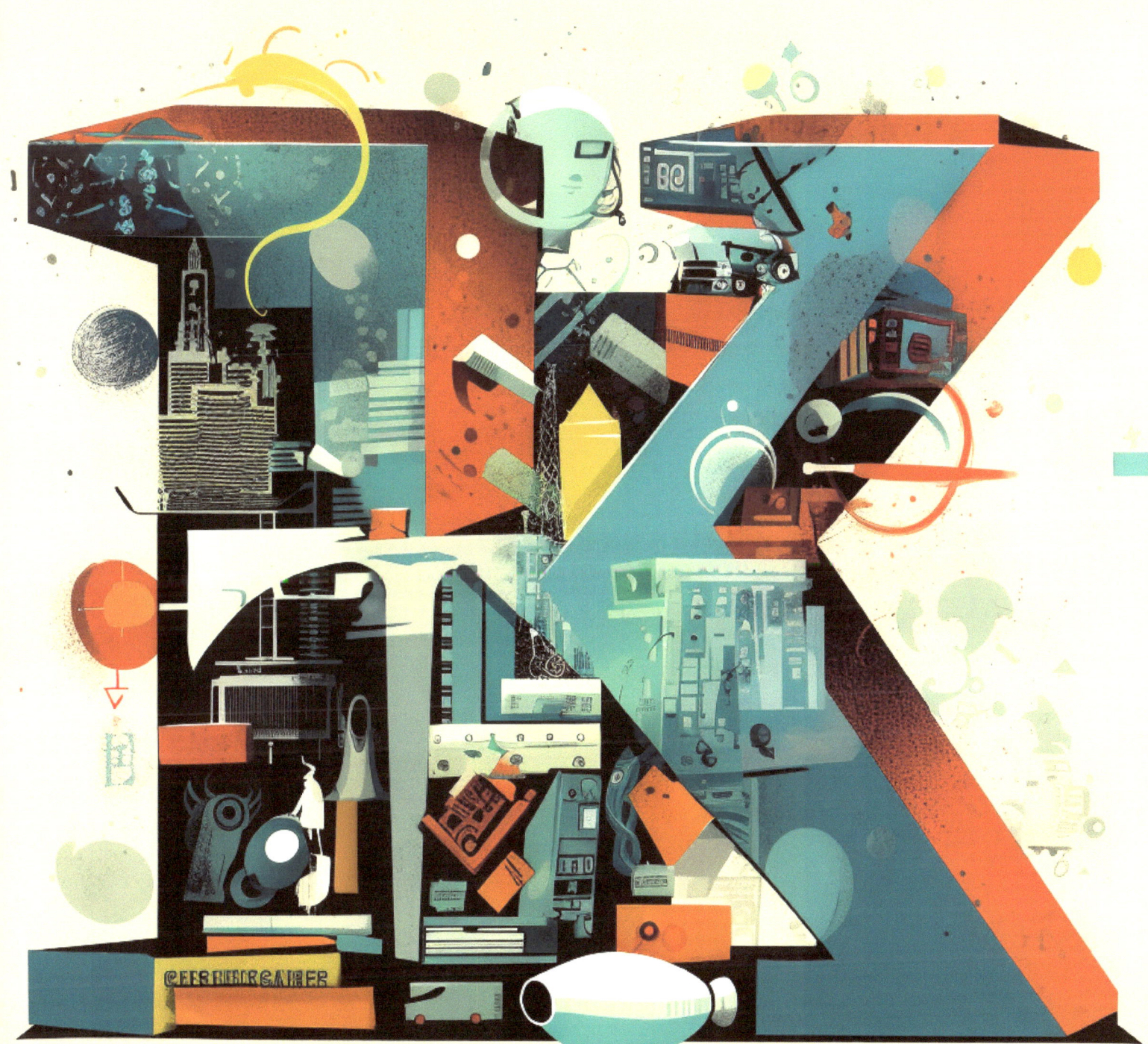

L is for Language, AI can speak,
It can translate, and be very unique.

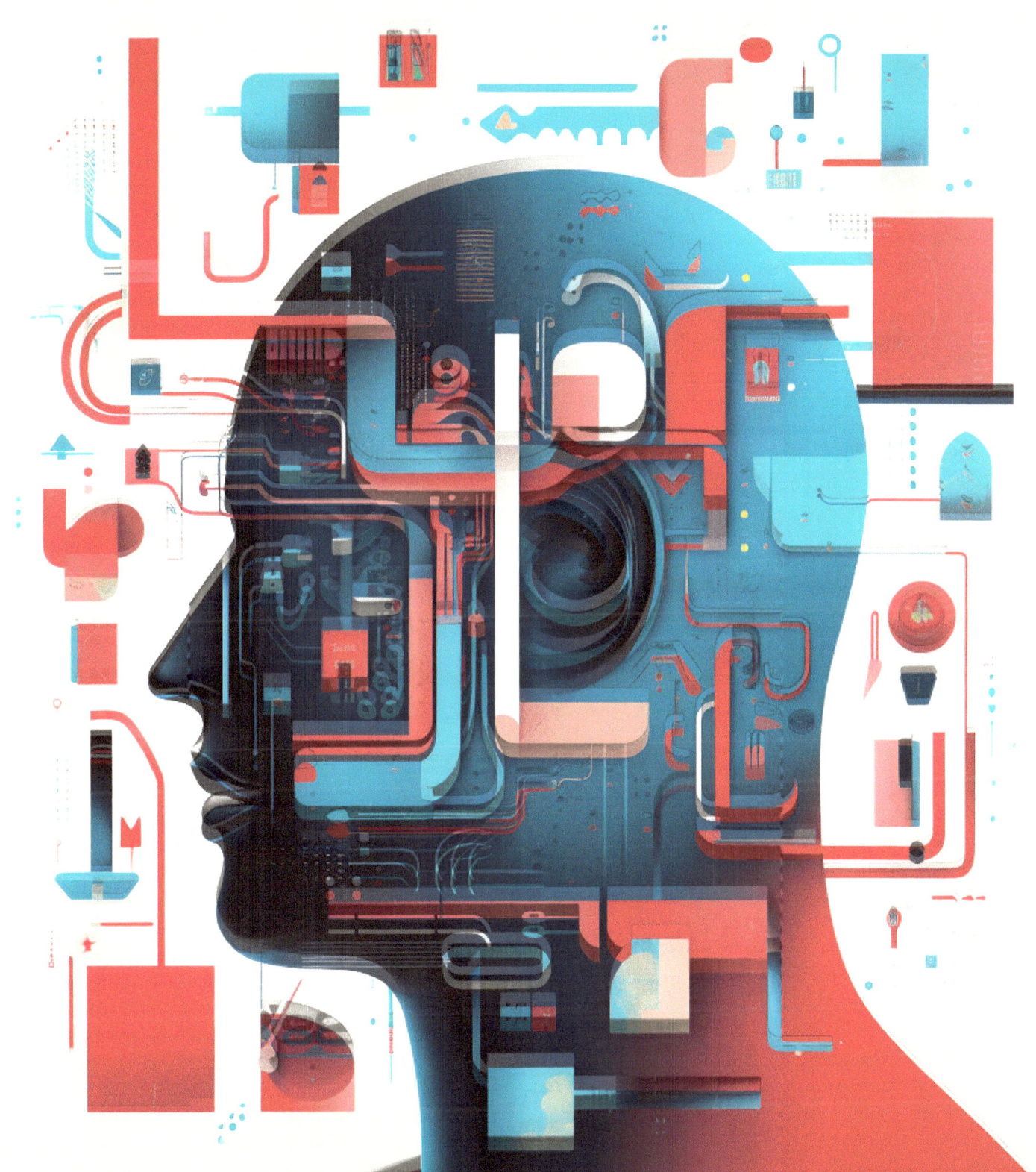

M is for Machine Learning,
AI can train itself, without human tutoring.

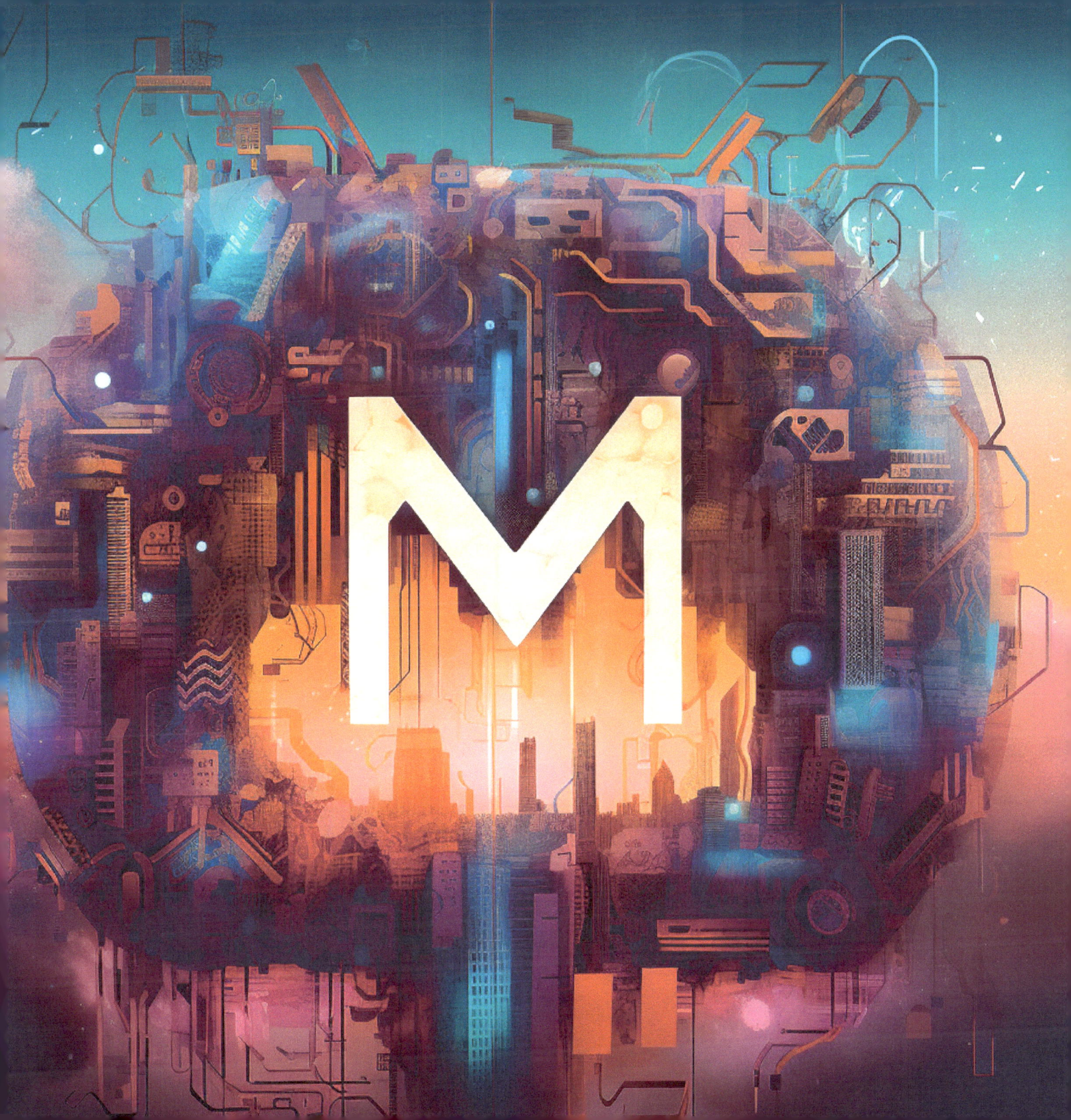

N is for Neural Network,
AI can learn, and pattern detect.

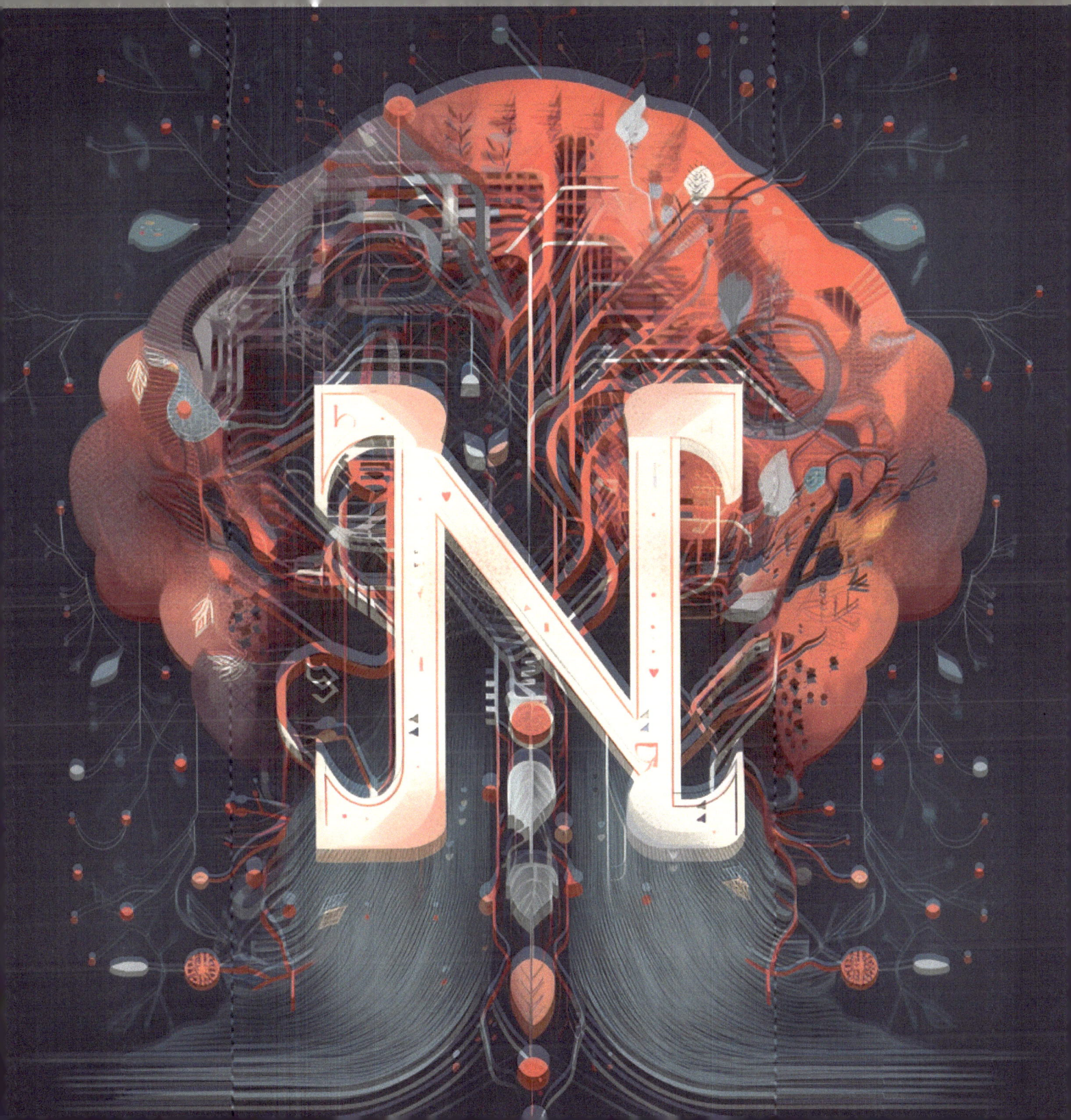

O is for Optimization,
AI can improve, with each iteration.

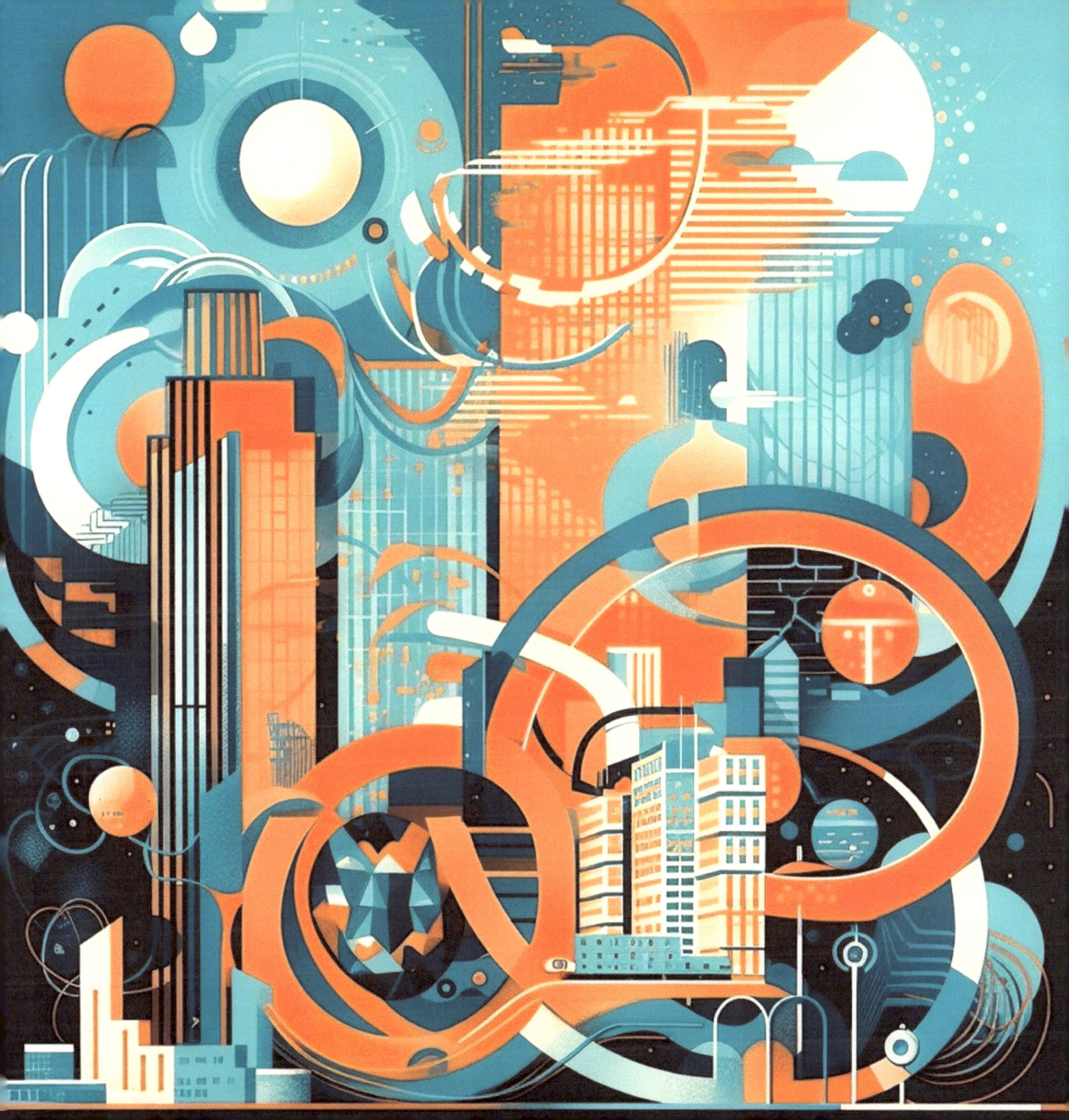

P is for Predictive Analytics;
AI can forecast, and give us the basics.

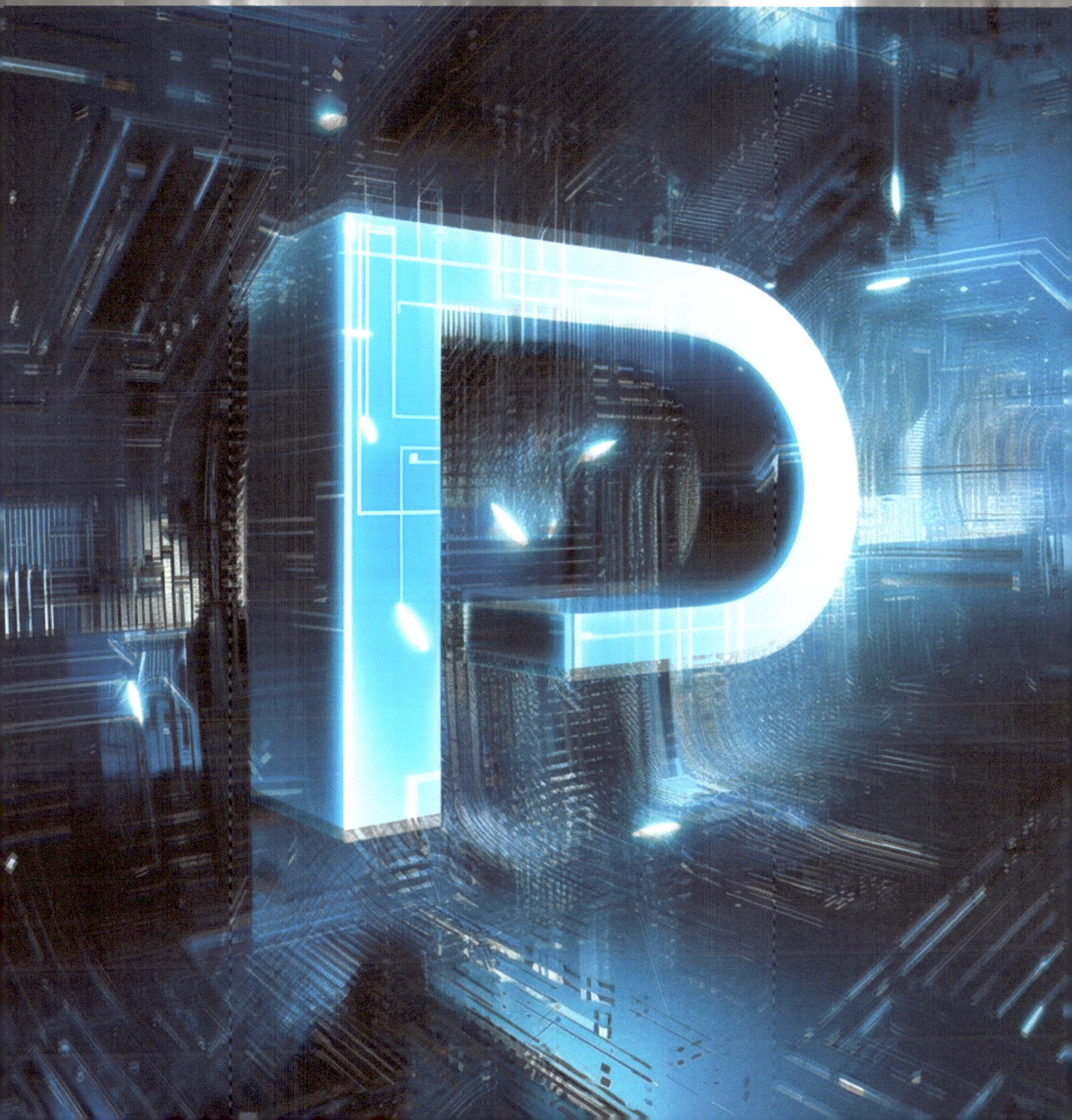

Q is for Quantum Computing,
AI can process, with faster computing.

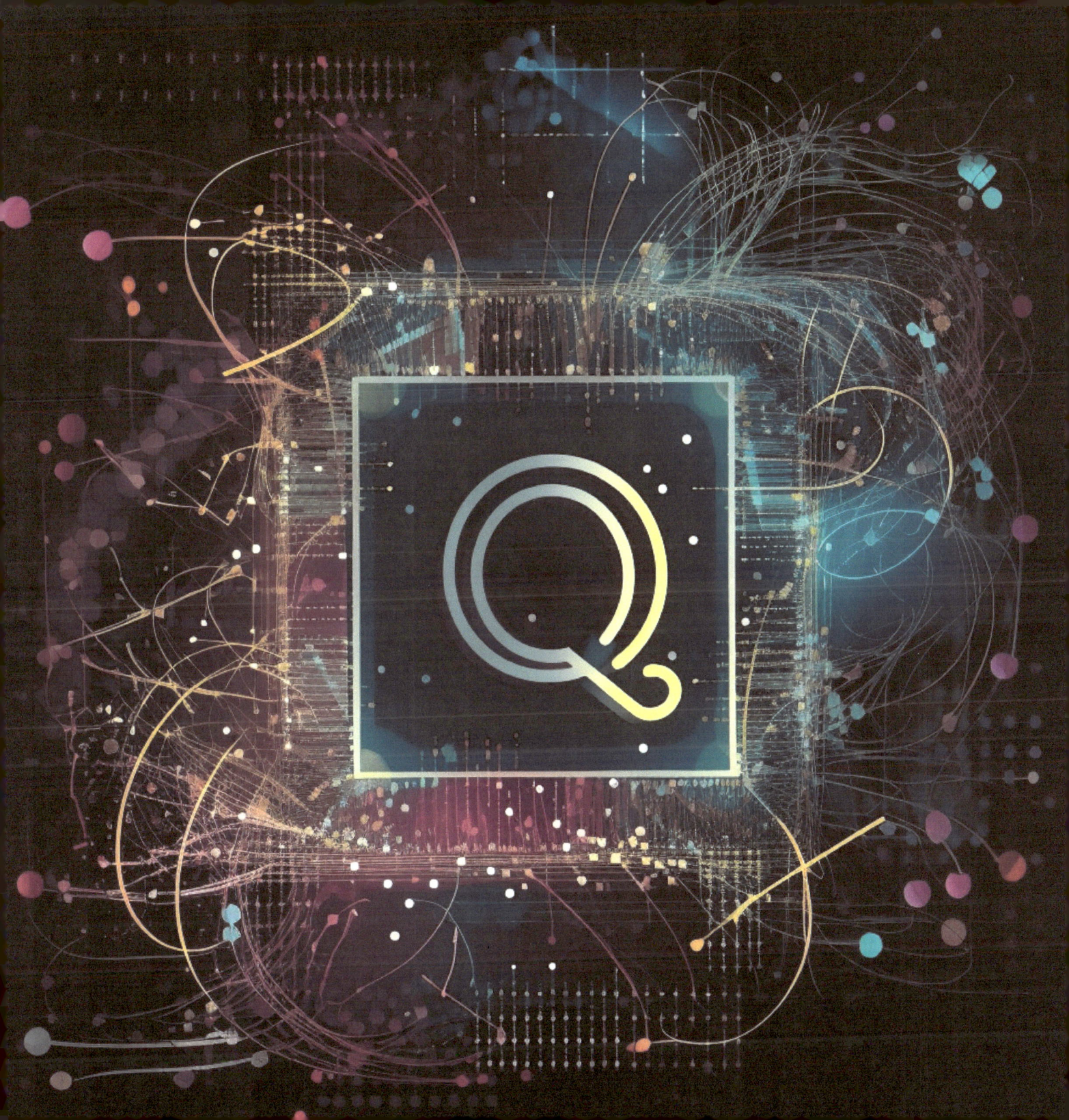

R is for Robotics,
AI can control, and work with mechanics.

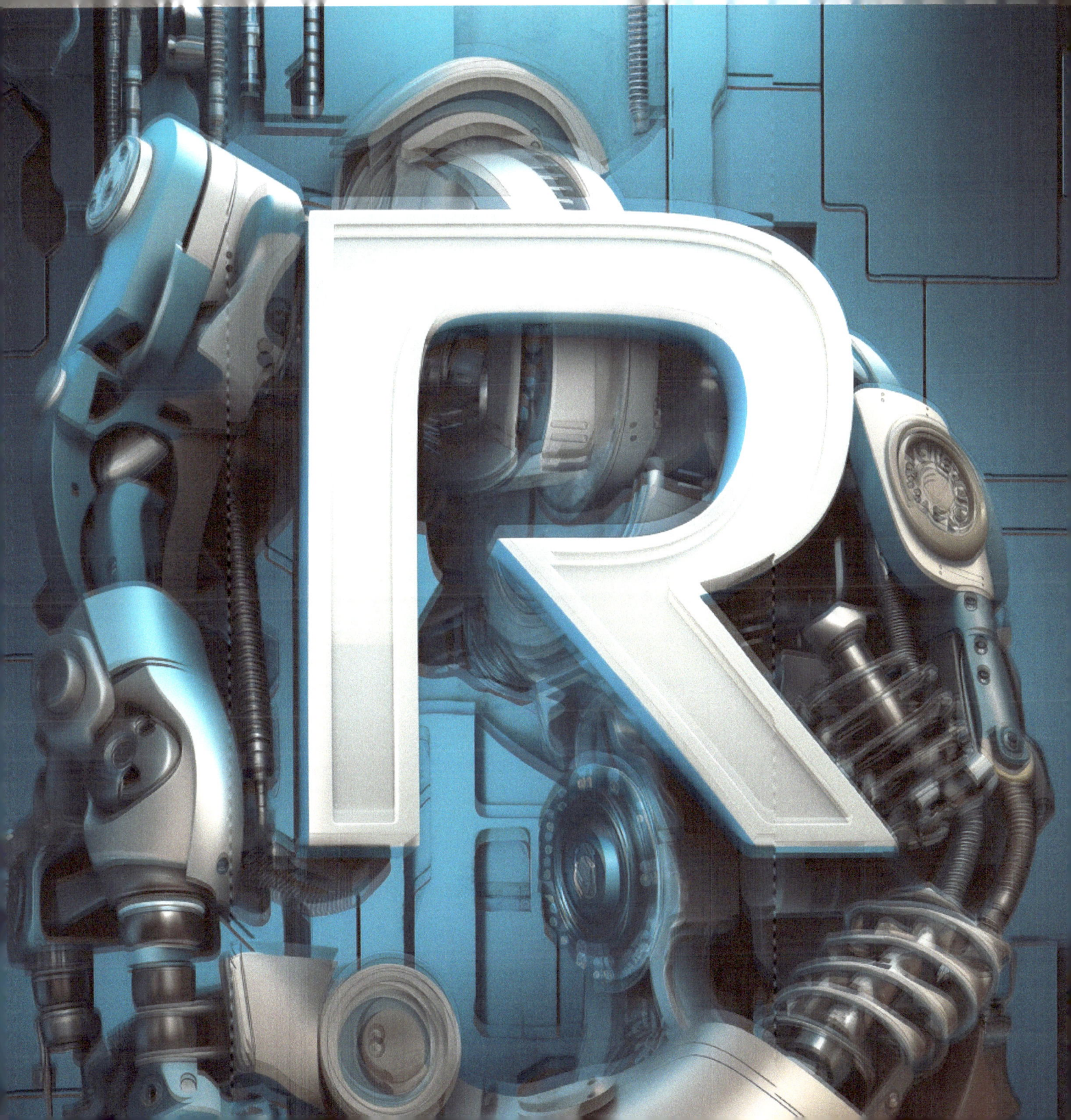

S is for Smart Home,
AI can make it happen, no need to roam.

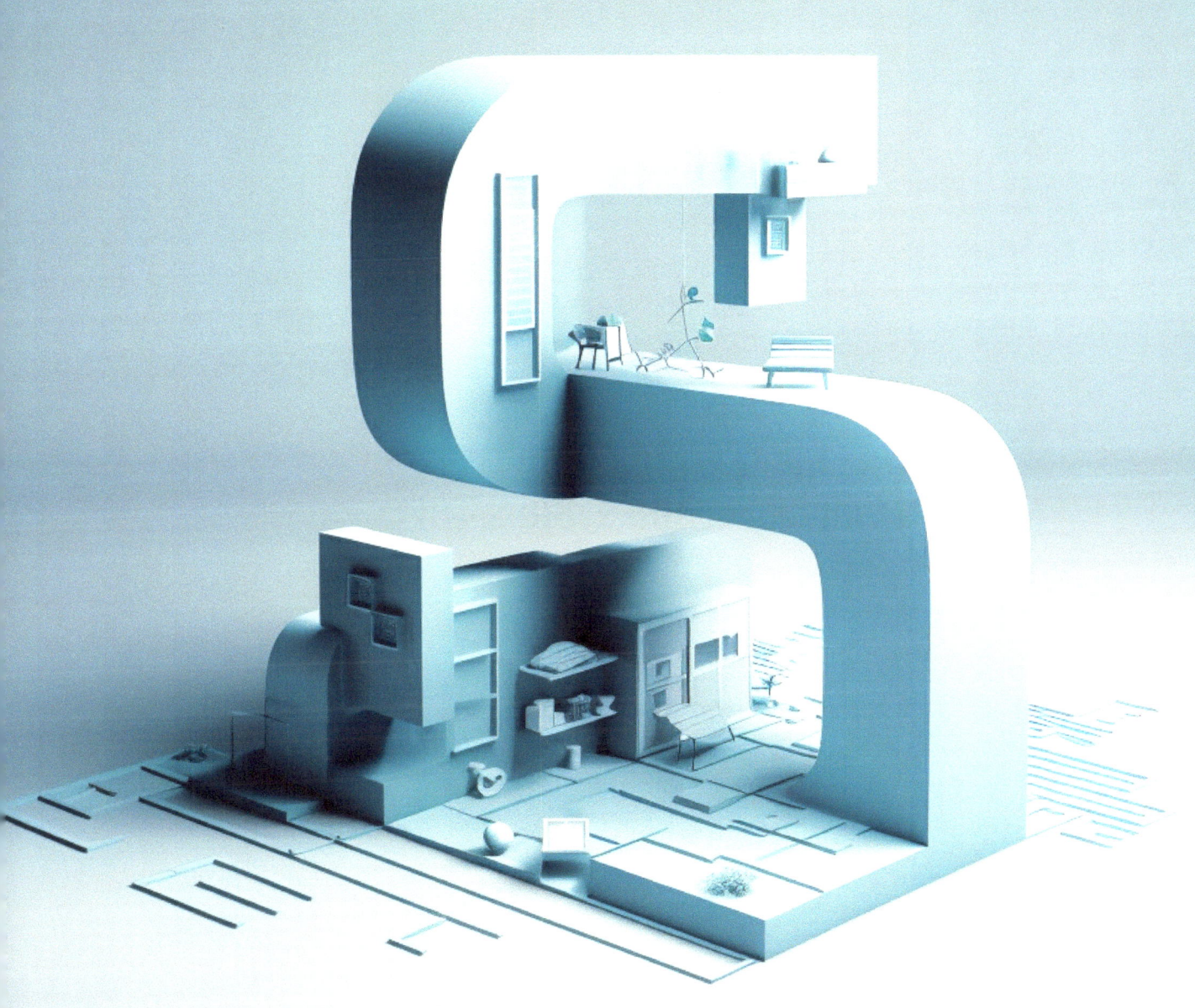

T is for Training Data,
AI can learn, and avoid errors.

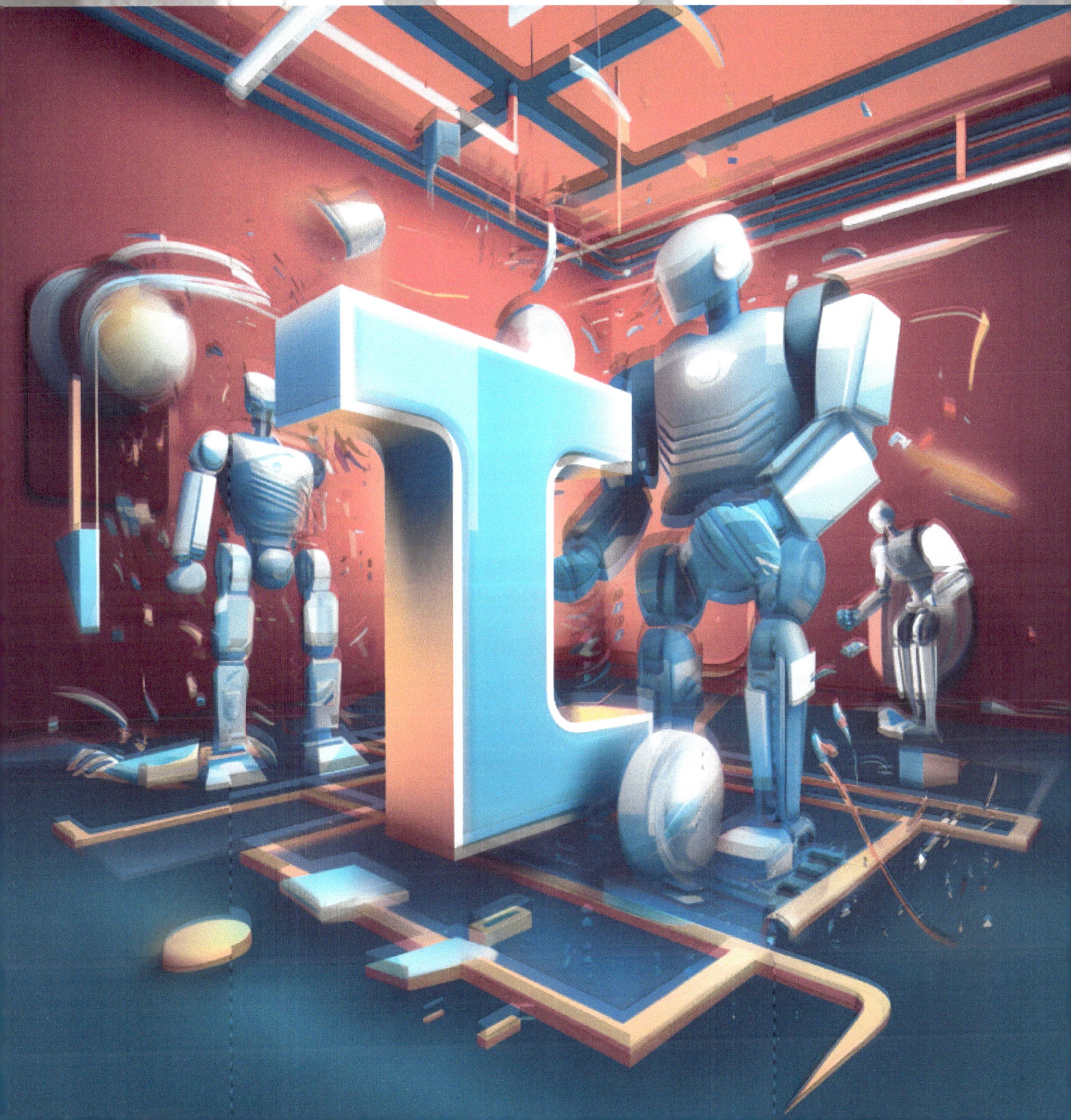

U is for Unsupervised Learning,
AI can self-learn, and be so appealing.

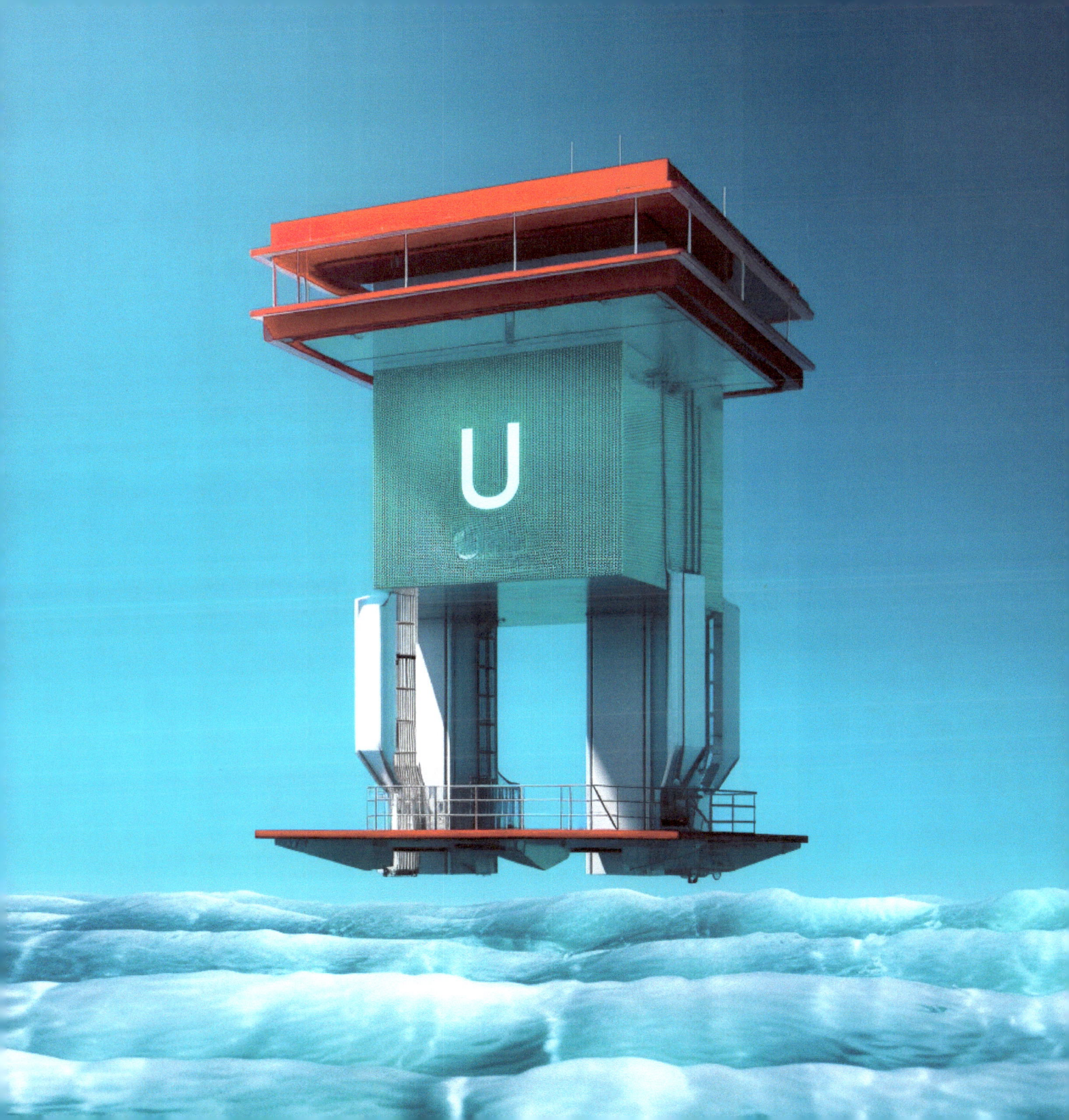

V is for Virtual Assistants,
AI can assist, and be so constant.

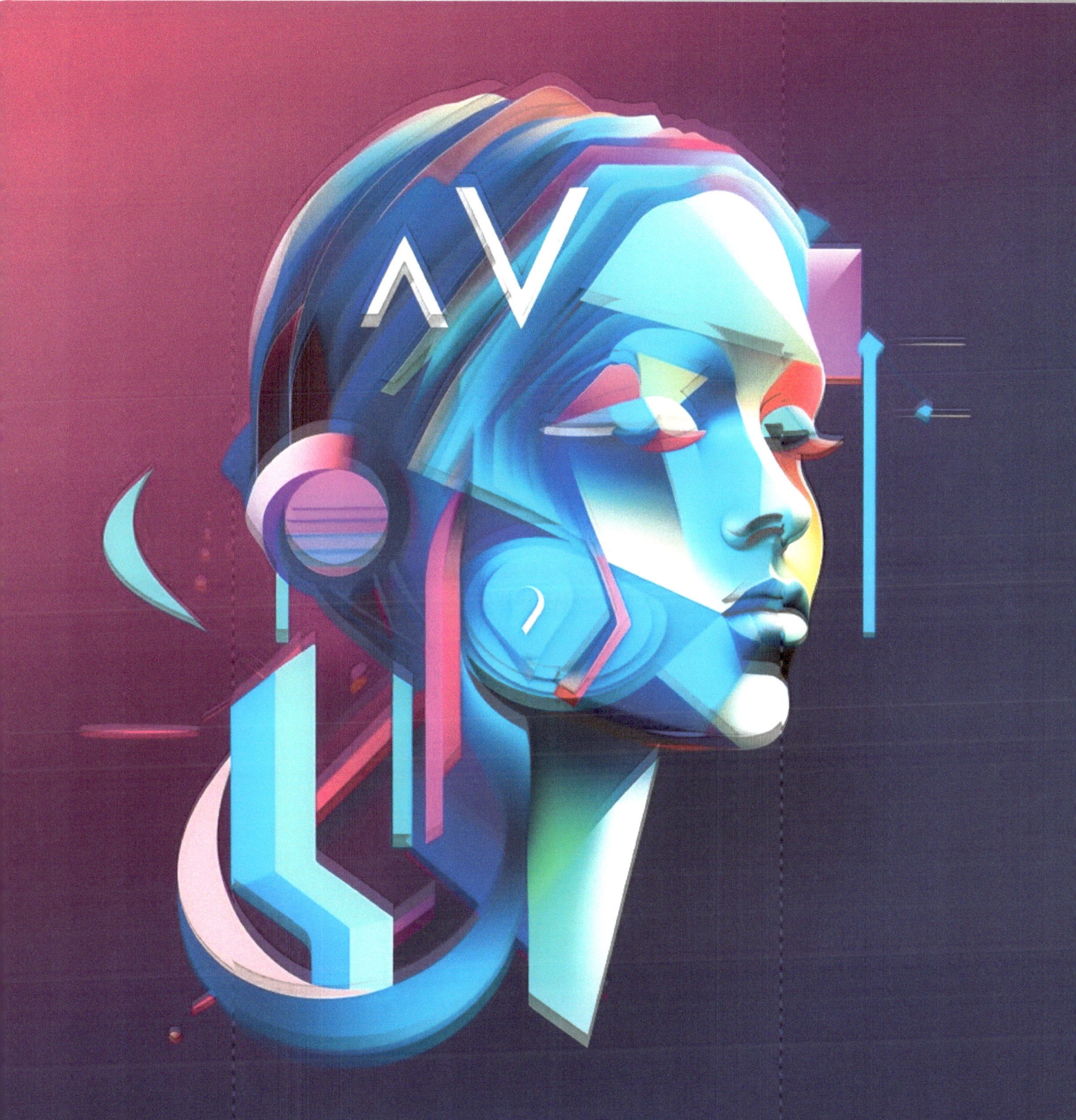

W is for Web Crawling,
AI can search, and find the calling.

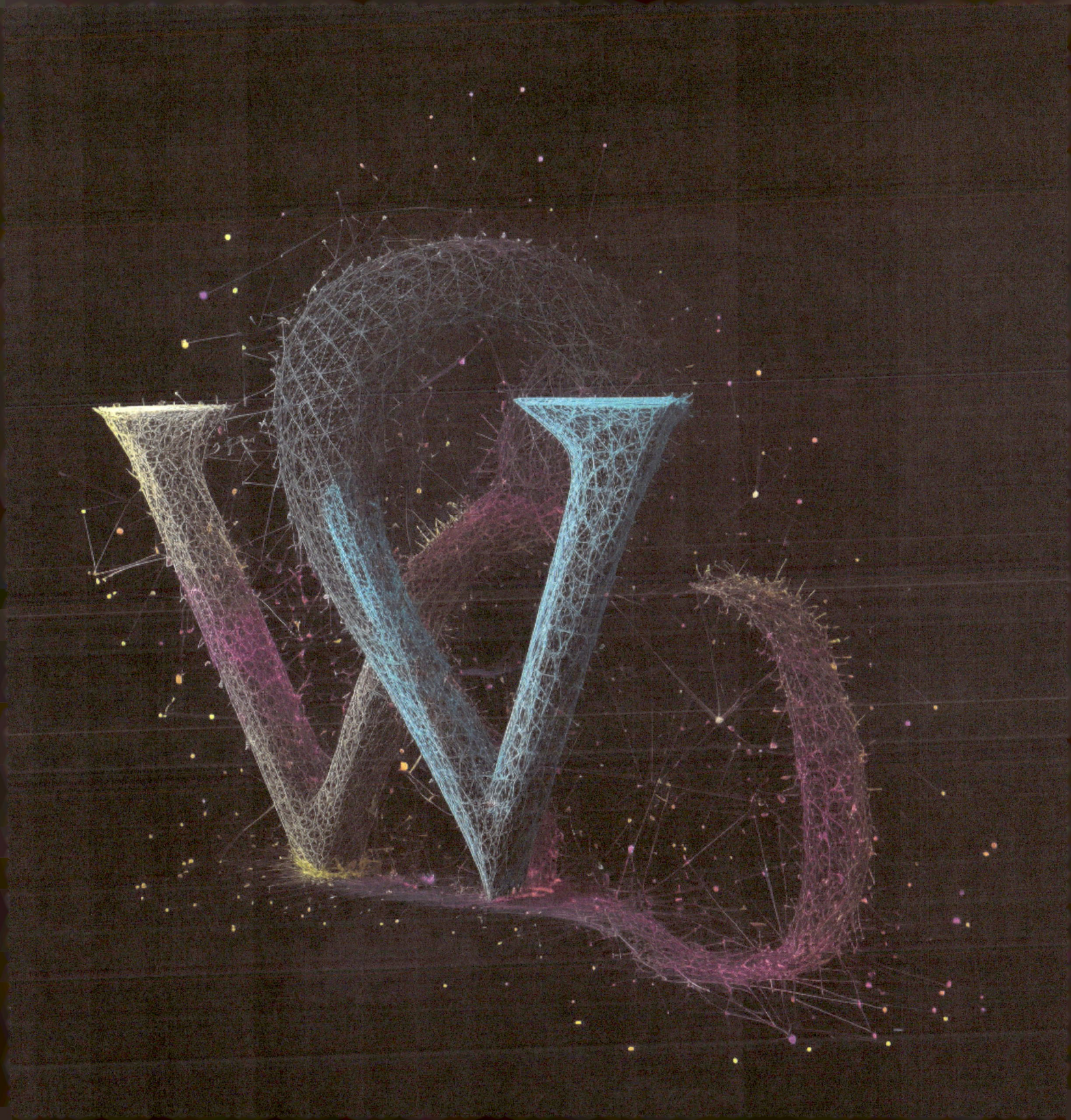

X is for X-Ray Scans,
AI can analyze, and give us a chance.

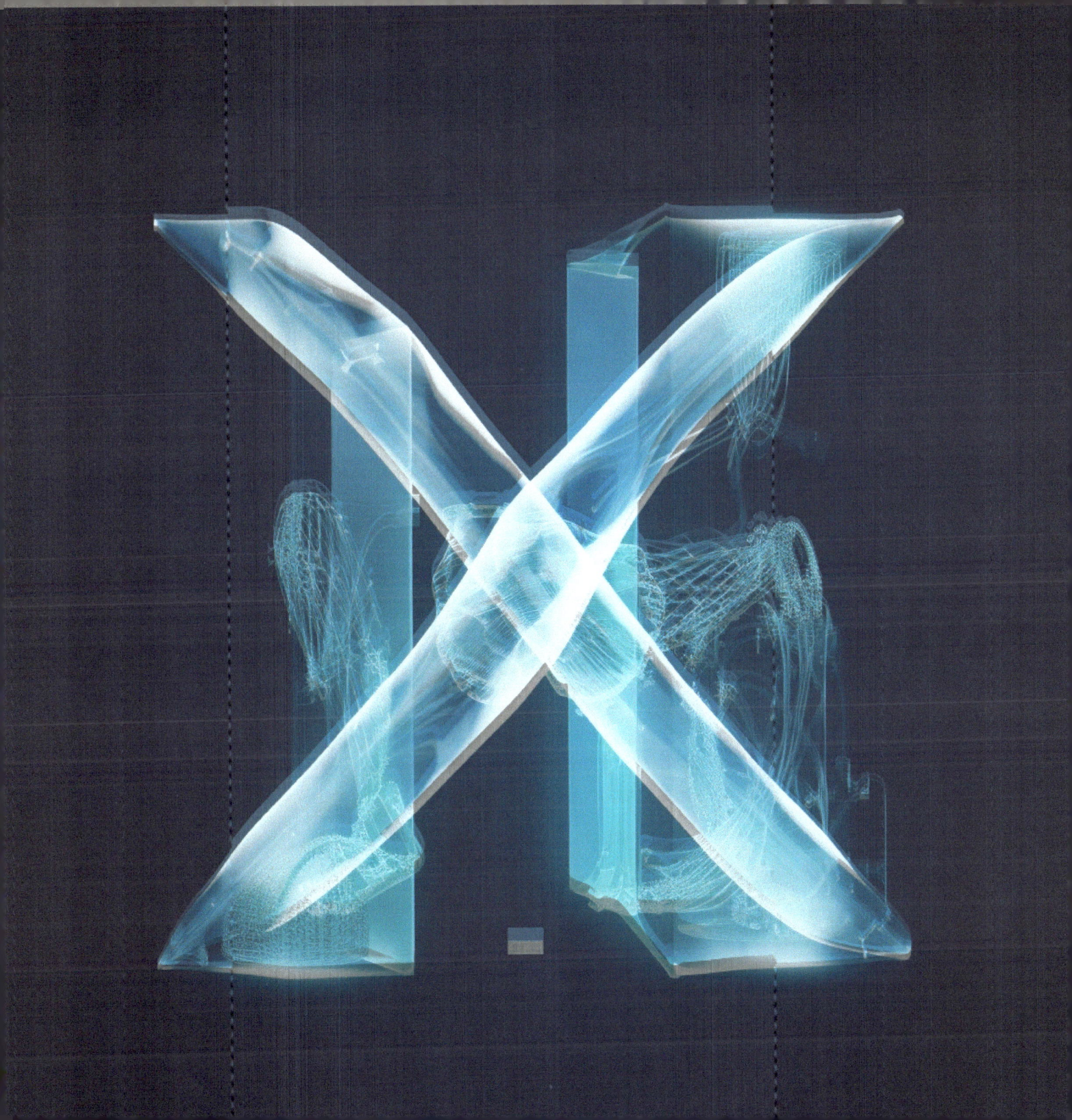

Y is for You and I,
AI can help, and make us thrive.

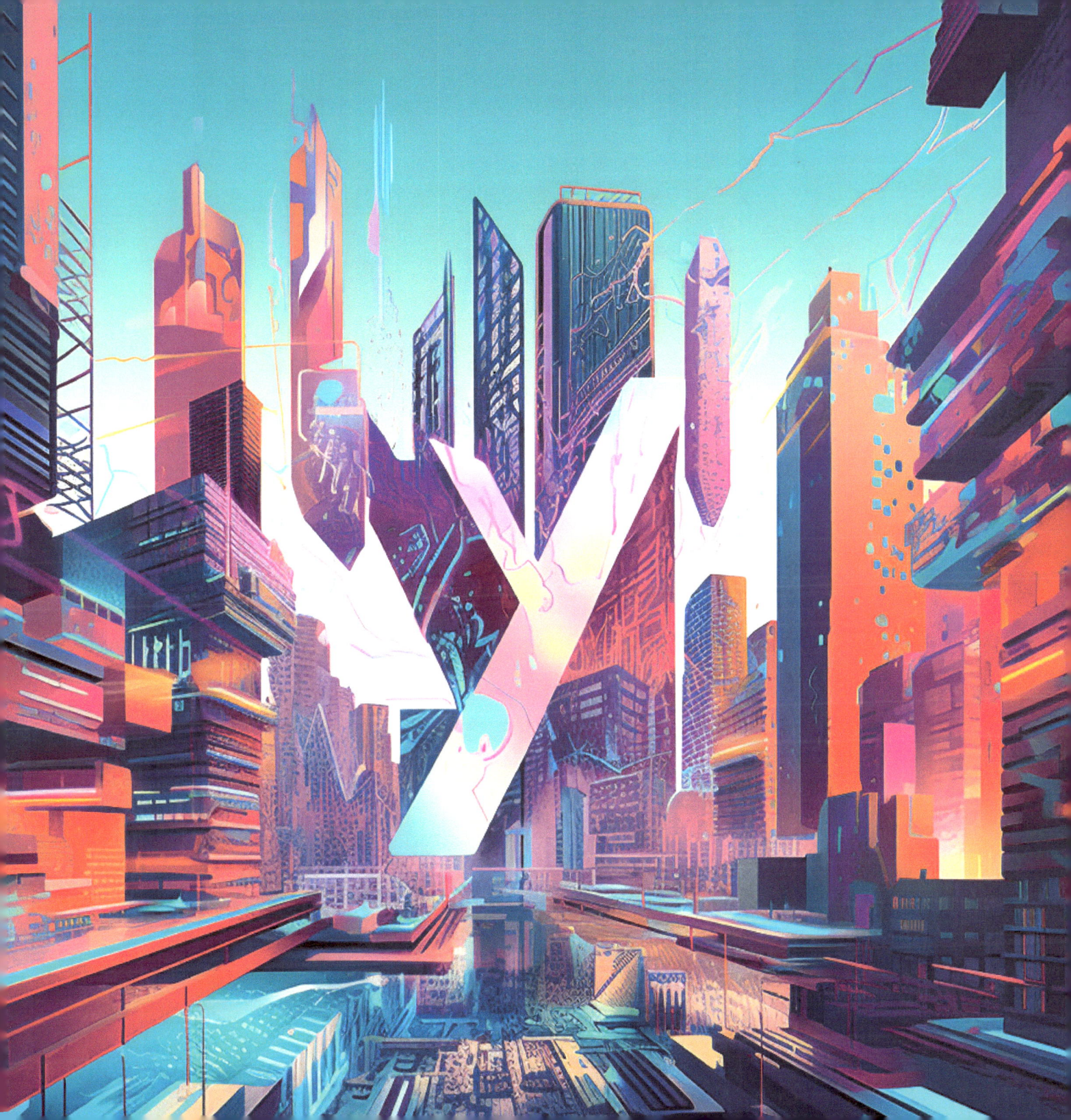

Z is for Zero-One Code,
AI can compute, and break the code.

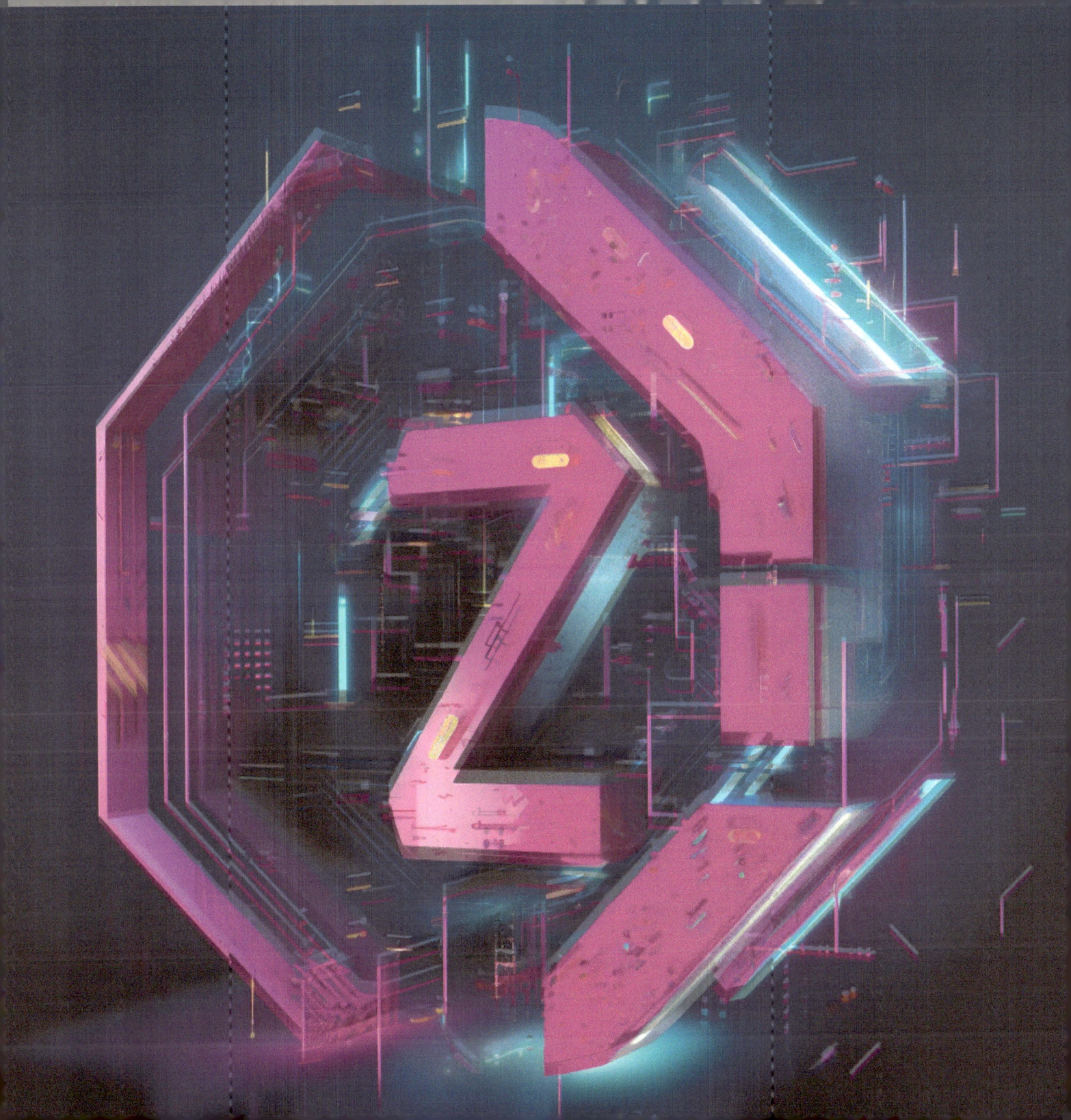

The End

www.ingramcontent.com/pod-product-compliance
Lightning Source LLC
Chambersburg PA
CBHW051954210526
45473CB00030B/2101